CASUAL

RACISM

&

INVISIBLE

BIAS

Written by

Guerdie Chery-Mesilas

I dedicate this book to my family. My grandmother always told me, "Being a good person never happens by accident; it takes work and dedication." We are not supposed to leave this world the way we found it. We must make it better. You may not notice the difference that you are making due to lack of praise or validation, but remain good, practice being a good person. Some people put their lives on the line every day to help others; they go unnoticed because they did not make the front-page news or go viral on social media. Know that your efforts to change a life or make someone's day better have an impact.

As a human on planet Earth, we are more connected than most of us think. We are our brother's keeper, whether we like it or not. Until we start treating each other with respect and dignity, our world will suffer. Every human cause on justice, equality, respect, and love, is a common cause that should unite and concern all of us, regardless of who is affected. [1]Mark 3:25 KJV, "If a house is divided against itself, that house cannot stand." It is also true of a country. If it is divided, it will fall. A nation divided will not survive. Unity and diversity give strength and power to conquer and subdue all outside forces. We all have one common enemy, and it is not each other. Love one another in all we do, regardless of race, ethnicity, class, and social status.

---

[1] *Holy Bible, New International Version. Biblical Inc. Publishing House, 2011.*

Table of Contents

pg. 5 Guerdie Chery-Mesilas

INTRODUCTION:

I wish I could tell you a way to avoid casual racism and invisible biases. Their effect ranges from minor annoyances for some to major devastation for others. There is no formula or ten-steps program to follow.

Casual racism is one form of racism that involves negative stereotypes of a group and uses it as ordinary words, sometimes without knowing or intending to hurt others. There are other times it is with malicious intent. They both accomplish the same goal: to hurt or upset the receiver.

Invisible biases are the unconscious racism that condition our decisions. They remained hidden yet powerful enough to affect our understanding, actions, and decisions. Invisible biases intertwine with culture and everyday life from school, work, and government policies. The implications are endless. Their impact can range from minor to major life-changing events and sometimes death.

There are countless books and movies about racism that depict the hard lives of slaves, and even after slavery ended, Black people struggled for years, fighting for acceptance and equality. The struggles are still there and have a way of reinventing themselves; they take on different forms. It can be challenging to prove discrimination unless you have solid, verifiable proof. It is nearly impossible to determine the invisible biases that exist which guide policies and decision-making processes.

Racism is a learned behavior and is deeply rooted within us. If you are not actively working on being anti-racist by changing how you think and question existing policies that you are following, you most likely have discriminated against someone. White people do benefit from a system that privileged them over Black people, whether they acknowledge it or not, and should not apologize for it. However, knowledge of unfairness and not taking a stand against it is complicity.

Maya Angelou said, "[2]If you're not angry, you're either a stone, or you're too sick to be angry. You should be angry. You must not be bitter. Bitterness is like cancer. It eats upon the host. It doesn't do anything to the object of its displeasure. So, use that anger. You write it. You paint it. You dance it. You do everything about it. You talk it. Never stop talking it." Therefore, I am writing it.

---

[2] *Processing anger: A conversation with Dr. Maya Angelou & Dave Chappelle.* (2016, December 15).

PART I

TELL
THE
TRUTH

"You shall not give false testimony against your neighbor."

[3](Exodus 20:16 NIV)

---

[3] *Holy Bible, New International Version. Biblical Inc. Publishing House, 2011.*

Combating casual racism emanating from systemic racism based on the philosophy that one race is superior to another, is an individual effort. We must act honestly in our daily dealing with others to prevent invisible biases from taking control. For instance, when a white person reports an incident at work or to the local authorities, they most likely, believed them and made decisions based on the information received. Race should not be a determining factor to be honest or to do the right thing.

There is an incident that happened to me a few years ago. A supervisor decided to lie about a lost item, and the management believed his account of the event without proof. His words were enough and almost changed the course of my life. I worked at a place where inclusion, ethics, and workplace safety were priorities. There were all forms of communication, emails, memos, flyers, and courses to remind everyone to do the right thing. Unfortunately, daily practice differed significantly from what was on paper. Some people thought they were above the rules and could get away with bad behavior, and sometimes they did. Their management styles, in effect, were founded on invisible biases against others. They discriminated against others and succeeded in doing so easily with no repercussions. The story below did happen; I omitted the names of people involved and used their titles to explain what transpired.

On Friday, April 3, 2009, I changed my shift with another employee and worked during the afternoon shift from 3 p.m. until 11 p.m. with supervisor 1. Management had made some changes to our regular duties by incorporating other sections, which is why I found myself working with supervisor 1 in his area. We also worked closely with the police department. Late that night, a police officer called and reported they had found lost property in building 1. I received a call from the radio to pick up the items. I proceeded to do so. The next step was to store the items in the lost-and-found office. Since I do not usually perform that task and do not know if I had access to the office, I called supervisor 1 on the radio to assist with granting access to the lost-and-found office.

He accessed the office by swiping his badge from the back door and made his way to the front door to open it for me. We both sat in the room and filled out the paper describing the found items. The items were a bag with a professional camera and another bag with little girl toys. We placed them on the shelf.

Supervisor 1 suggested checking my access to the room. He thought it would be more efficient in the future. I could complete this task without the need to call a supervisor. Instead of exiting from the front door, we both swiped our badges to exit through the back door. My card worked; I did have access to the room. We both made our way back to our main office in a different building. Shortly after, I left work at 11:00 p.m. and went home. I was on vacation for over a week.

During my time off on Tuesday, April 7th, I received a phone call from the police department. The person on the line was vague and brief. He wanted to know where we kept lost-and-found items. I advised him that all found property was placed in the lost-and-found office. I was not at work and would be unable to help. He needed to contact the control center; they could put him in touch with the lost-and-found office or the supervisor on shift for assistance. He did not say anything else; the call ended.

On Wednesday, April 8th, supervisor 1 called me and stated my vacation was not approved; I needed to come back to work. I replied to him that the manager in charge of scheduling confirmed my time off, and I had the paperwork to prove it. If he made an error, upon my return, I would discuss it with him. Supervisor 1 was furious on the phone and started complaining about not having enough staff, and that I was disobeying a directive to come back to work. The call ended, and I stayed on my vacation.

I went back to work on Wednesday, April 15, 2009. After an hour of being on shift, I was approached by supervisor 2, wanting to have a word with me in private. I followed him to an office. He advised me the police department wanted to talk to me. I asked him if he knew why. He stated he was not sure, that they might have some questions regarding lost-and-found property. I asked him if he had a name and number of who needed to talk to me. He said no, they wanted to see me in person. I told him no problem and asked him to give me an hour to finish a few things; then I would make my way to their office in building 2; I knew where the office is. He replied, no, I have to take you there now. I followed him to the car, where he drove me to their location and handed me over to a female detective.

When I arrived in the office of the police department, it looked like a conference room, but it was an interrogating room. The female detective greeted me and asked me to sit down. She started by making small conversation, like how are you, which shift are you working, and stated she was waiting for the other detectives to arrive. Ten to fifteen minutes later, two male detectives entered the room and greeted me. One of them handed me a piece of paper to read. As I started to read it, I realized it was the Miranda rights, something I knew from watching the TV series *Law & Order;* other than that, I would not even know what it was. One detective asked if I understood what I read, I told him that I did not, that it said Myranda rights on top, and from watching TV, it was what you said to people before arresting them.

One detective explained to me that I was not in trouble; this was standard procedure for them before they could start asking me questions. They had to make sure I understood my rights. I did not have to talk to them, and I could ask for a lawyer. I asked them why would I ask for a lawyer when I did not know why I was there? I begged them to please let me know why I was here. I did not get an answer; they were all looking at me. I proceeded to tell them that if they needed my help to investigate something that happened, I would talk to them.

They started by asking personal questions, and they each took turns asking the same things. For instance, what was my name, phone, address, marital status, how long had I been in the United States and how long had I been working for this current company, where did I work before, if I had any children. One of them would interrupt with small talk about the temperature, then back to the personal question over and over. That went on for a good forty-five minutes, and each time I answered the same thing. I got tired of it, and that was when I confronted them, saying they kept asking me the same questions over and over about my family and personal information. My answers were not going to change. I needed to know what was going on and why I was there.

One detective stated, "You are here because on the night of April 3rd, you picked up found property from a police officer, and the lost-and-found are not able to provide the item to the owner. The owner filed a report, and we investigated the disappearance of the property, and it traced back to you." I asked them how could that be, because after I picked up the items from the police officer, I secured them in the lost-and-found office and left work shortly after. I had been out on vacation from that night, and this was my first day back to work.

One detective exclaimed, "Upon the investigation, supervisor 1 reported you probably went back to the lost-and-found office and took the item, which was a professional camera." I explained to the detectives I was on vacation for over a week. After I left on the night of April 3rd, I did not come back until today, April 15th. I asked them, other than what supervisor 1 reported, what type of investigation was conducted that led them to me. One of the detectives said they talked to the police officer, who confirmed he gave me the items, and saw it on the video in building 1 when the handoff occurred. They also went in the lost-and-found office where the found property was, and someone with access to the room removed it.

I replied, "Based on the word of supervisor 1, you determined that I am your thief." They answered that yes because we two were the only two people that came in contact with the found property that night, and he said I probably went back and took it.

I proceeded to explain how to access the lost-and-found office. A badging system regulated access to the office. The only way to bypass it was if, someone from inside the office, physically opened the front door for you. The only way to go inside the office was to swipe your badge from the back door of the room. My next question was if they had checked the ID swiped of everyone that went in that room. The answer was "No." I proceeded by saying a surveillance camera monitored the place. Had they reviewed the footage of what went on in the lost-and-found office starting from the night of April 3rd? The answer again was no, because no one advised them of the camera in the room.

I told them unless I had the gift of invisibility, that was the only way I could access the lost-and-found office unnoticed to steal the found property and not leave a trace behind.

One detective replied, "Still, the theft happened; someone switched the professional camera that was in the bag with an older model. I reasoned with him. How could I swap a camera when I did not even own one? I advised them to check my ID swipe and camera footage from the room, since they had not done so, but here I was being interrogated as guilty until I could prove my innocence, and they kept insisting I did it.

Management from my department that were involved in the investigation neglected to advise the detectives of the camera in the room that monitored it and provide them access to the footage. One detective asked me if I would be willing to go back to the lost-and-found office with them, to show them the facts that I presented to them. I agreed to follow them.

I showed and reenacted what we did the night of April 3. I pointed to the camera that monitored the room, and it covered the whole area. One detective pointed to a bag that was supposed to be the found property that contained a camera. One of the detectives asked me to pick up and open the bag to confirm if it was the one from that night. I told them it had been a few days since I last saw the found property, but this one did not look like the one the police officer gave me. I closed the bag and placed it back on the self.

We all left the room the same way we came in. While outside of the room, one of the detectives instructed me that they would not escort me back to building 2. I could go back to work but not leave the premises, in case I was needed again for more questioning. I explained to them that when my shift was over at 11:00 p.m., I would go home. After that time, they could call me because they had my phone number.

I did not receive a call back from the detectives. Around 11:02 p.m., when my shift was over, I was making my way to my car from the parking lot. Supervisor 3 started talking to me and said, "By the way, have you heard someone got fired tonight for stealing?" I asked who got fired; he proceeded to tell me that supervisor 1 got fired for stealing. The Directors D1, D2 and Managers M1, M2, and PIO (public information officer) and a few other people from management were all here tonight along with the media. The police arrested supervisor 1, and his picture was on the news all night and would make the front page of the local paper the next day. I stopped and looked at him without saying a word; I felt my soul leaving my body. I was in a state of shock. I drove home, and I was shaking; I did not recall how I made it there.

When I got home, I started to replay what just happened. The arrest of supervisor 1, the newspaper, the TV station, and the directors and managers were all there for my arrest. They believed supervisor 1's account of the story. After all, he had been there for years, and he was an older white man. All the people in the story had one thing in common: they were all white except supervisor 2, who was instructed to drive me and handed me over to the detectives. They all neglected to advise the detectives of crucial information that would have solved the case during the investigation or lack thereof.

I am not sure in what setting supervisor 1 told his side of the story that accused me of being the thief. However, I am sure it was not after he was informed of his Miranda rights. I also realized the paper was handed to me to read because I was an immigrant with an accent; they had to make sure I read my rights and understood it to avoid a lack of comprehension of the English language. Was it done because I was a Black woman or an easy target, or was the sole motivation to get rid of me? Due to their casual racism and invisible biases of thinking, Black people are all criminals. They neglected to pass on vital information and acted on a lie. I could have lost my freedom, my family, and my reputation.

Since I did not usually work in that area, I had to find out if that was standard procedure. I spoke with employees who had been there for years. They told me they had never seen such enthusiasm and group effort to get someone arrested for lost-and-found property that went missing. I stayed up nights after nights, replaying the events in my head; I had so many questions.

Why did supervisor 1 lie to everyone?

Why did he call me at home to come back and lie about being short-staffed?

Why were the detectives misinformed?

Why weren't all the facts and information provided to the detectives so they could conduct a proper investigation?

Why was the media there?

Why were all the directors present?

Why was the presence of so many people from management necessary?

My many Whys went without answers. I called the department in charge of the employee's well-being. I set up an appointment to speak with a psychologist. I was having difficulty reconciling the action of supervisor 1 as the sole work of a sociopath. Was the well-orchestrated arrest on TV a group effort to hurt one person while withholding proof that could have solved the case? One thing was clear: they were not after the truth, because they would not have left one stone unturned.

The phycologist told me that I was handling it well; the bright side was no harm was done because I did not get arrested. I should go back to work and talk to the managers involved and ask why they did not provide vital information to the detectives. I followed his advice and went back to work and requested to see the managers and directors involved. Only one manager and one director showed up. I asked them if it was safe for me to continue working there. They advised me that they were acting on the information received and when I asked why information pertinent to the case was not passed on to the detectives. Since the manager that had access to the footage did not show up, I did not get an answer. When I had a chance to see that manager, I asked him the same question; he told me it was an ongoing investigation. He did not want to interfere unless the detectives asked for it. I was more confused that this man knew the truth and was willing to let me go to jail.

In the end, I never received an apology from any of the managers or directors or an explanation of how they arrested supervisor 1, and what led them to mobilize the media to cover the arrest for a minor incident. Later, through other employees who believed what happened was outrageous, I was told that when the detectives arrested supervisor 1 and told him they were unable to establish a connection with me returning to the lost-and-found office to switch the camera, supervisor 1 admitted he was guilty; he switched the professional camera with an older model he had. In his attempt to avoid the arrest, he mentioned taking the camera home so he could buy one for his wife. He went to his car and gave the original camera back to the detectives.

A few months later, I also found out supervisor 1 sued the company for defamation of character, and that he had improperly borrowed the camera and did not steal it. As a result, he lost his job and reputation and was seeking compensation. I have no idea how they settled with him.

After the incident, the microaggression that followed was unbearable. One day, a soft-spoken white woman walked up to me and said, "You were involved in the arrest of supervisor 1." I looked at her, and before I had a chance to answer, she said, "well he was a good, respectable, Christian man; it is a shame what happened to him. I still do not think he did it." I stood there, unable to move and feeling embarrassed, not for me but for her. I replied to her, "You do know he returned the stolen property." I walked away from her before the conversation got worse; I had a feeling she had more to say to me.

The harassment from people asking me what had happened just to tell me I was the one that should have been arrested was overwhelming. If I had done anything before to make these people hate me or doubt my innocence, it would make sense to me why they would want me to get arrested. I did not know what to do with these prejudiced minds how could they still be in doubt after a white man accused a Black woman of stealing something that he was guilty of stealing and returned the stolen property?

I wanted to leave, but finding other employment had proven very difficult. I still had to provide for my family. I stayed and endured countless moments of being targeted, experienced disparate treatments, discrimination, harassment, retaliation, and retribution that I could not prove happened or was done with malice.

The story above may seem an isolated event that only happens to people who are not careful or are stealing from their employer. I was a good employee and had not given any reason to be suspected of wrongdoing. Besides, no harm was done, which is what was said to me because I did not get arrested. However, I had to prove my innocence by providing information about the security system in place that could have solved the case rapidly. No one was on my side, the side of the truth. I had no one believing that I was not capable of stealing. I was not even granted the courtesy of a conversation without being Mirandized base on a one-person account of what occurred.

There are countless people in jail serving time for crimes they did not commit, and they were condemned without proof just based on lies by other people. Black people are often victimized by people thinking they are superior and have the moral high ground, and lied to send mothers, fathers, young men, and women to jail and destroyed their futures. I find it troublesome when told that no harm resulted from the incident. These experiences do not leave you. They stay and eat you inside and grow the type of fear and anxiety you never knew existed. Some people get bitter; others use it to get better.

Be better. [4]"You shall not give false
testimony against your neighbor" (Exodus
20:16 NIV).

---

[4] *Holy Bible, New International Version. Biblical Inc. Publishing House, 2011.*

pg. 32 Guerdie Chery-Mesilas

PART II

THE GOLDEN RULE

"So in everything, do to others what you would have them do to you" [5](Matthew 7:12 NIV)

---

[5] *Holy Bible, New International Version. Biblical Inc. Publishing House, 2011.*

pg. 34 Guerdie Chery-Mesilas

Many philosophers throughout time have made The Golden Rule a centerpiece or part of their life. People have heard and read about it for a long time. While some tend to practice it at home and in their everyday life, others may find it challenging to grasp the idea of treating others the same way as themselves.

The application of this law in all aspects of the American culture and government would mean no slavery. Let us just say after slavery, they realized the greed of wealth and slavery was costly to their souls. Let us be the Christian nation we are and practice what we preached; then, after the emancipation of the slave, Jim Crow laws and segregation would not be so prevalent in the south. After desegregation, Americans were more divided and unequally benefited from the wealth of the country.

Systematic racism established barriers that were impenetrable to Black families. It existed in housing, school systems, police departments, community service, and voting regulations that were put in place to keep the division, and the white race benefited from it.

The idea that systematic racism benefited White people and hindered Black people is a repulsive idea that most White people do not like to hear. It is in part due to a lack of understanding or the belief that they are not racist, which makes it impossible to accept as fact. In the words of Martin Luther King Jr., [6]"I do not see how we will ever solve the turbulent problem of race confronting our nation until there is an honest confrontation with it and a willing search for the truth and a willingness to admit the truth when we discover it."

The truth is slavery is not new; it has always existed throughout history. The Israelites were slaves in Egypt; the Romans also had slaves, just to name a few. However, slavery in America was different, and the difference is the ideology that the White race was somehow superior from the Black race. The labeling of the Black race as

---

[6] *The M.L. King speech.* (n.d.). 1968

inferior in mental capacity tried to justify the conflicted ideology of having slaves and all the atrocity that came with it.

When the Europeans came to America, the indigenous populations in the land in 1492 were estimated to be about 60 million. This number represented about 10% of the world population. Due to diseases they were not immune to, war, and harsh labor, by the 1600s, nearly 56 million died. According to PRI.org, that was 10% of the world population that died. Imagine if 10% of the world population vanished now, what would we call it? That was nothing short of genocide, whether we want to admit it or not.

No one wants to be the descendant of a group that committed genocide, I understand that much, and it is all about who is writing the history of the land. It will always reflect the nation that benefited from it as being the righteous one.

Let us move forward to the slavery of Africans. The genocide committed against the Black race over the centuries is yet to be acknowledged. So much so in our era right now, the old plantations are tourist attraction, turned into bed & breakfast that highlight how the plantation owners lived. They look like a great way to go back and be in touch with nature and experience the charm of the region. The martyred, the separated families, the raped, the sold, the slaves assassinated and tortured, will we ever know their names and their roots? The blatant refusal to acknowledge what took place in America is creating the situation that we are currently experiencing.

Only an honest look at the situation for what it was can clear the path for a better way of treating each other. What happened was wrong! History cannot be changed, but let us tell the story as truthfully as we can and eradicate from our mind that one man is superior to another based on the color of his skin. If you are of the White race, imagine that it was your ancestors that went through slavery. Imagine, feel, and then talk based on those feelings.

These conversations are not easy and have happened before. However, there is an underlining reason that is greater than race that continues to strengthen the issue. It is the economic factor. Remember, America had a war over slavery, the Civil War. Others will argue it was about state rights. But it was over keeping slaves as a source of revenue because the country was an industrial economy based on free labor.

When slavery was over, the plantations did not just close; they reinvented themselves to adjust and get the same result: free or cheap labor. They went from buying slaves to leasing them. Some of the blatant atrocities of slavery torture, rape, lynching, and the killing continued and got worse. There were laws put in place to target Black people, arrest them, and put them back in the same plantation where they used to work as slaves. For instance, the Vagrancy laws, which entailed mischief and insulting gestures, were only applied to the Black people. When the police arrested them for not having a job that they could not find in the first place, they were sent back to the same plantation to little or no pay. The plantation owners were now leasing the convict, and their well-being was not of any interest. They could always get more for free.

The Jim Crow laws in the south extended to every facet of life and became legal in 1896 when the Supreme Court ruled "these laws were legal because they reflected custom and tradition, preserve public peace and good order." In 1954, separate but equal laws Brown versus Board of Education happened. In 1956, a manifesto was signed by 101 out of 120 southern congressmen composed of 82 representatives and 19 senators to maintain the Jim Crow laws in the south, and resulted in more social injustice. African Americans are deprived of education, jobs, and a way to build wealth; yet America is a capitalistic society. It denied some of its citizens a way to enter and become a productive member of society. Capitalism is a political, social, and economic system based on private or

corporate ownership, and the free market.
The systematic racism and strategies put in
place by the government deliberately kept
most Blacks in overt poverty and bondage
all their lives from one generation to the
next.

In 1960, systematic racism took on a
new form; it reinvented itself. It became
about law and order. In 1968, law and order
were the centerpieces of President Richard
Nixon's campaign. Many politicians won
campaign elections on law and order and
enacted more stringent rules, and when
elected, they always tried to prove how
tough they were by making stricter rules.
The African Americans in America went
from enduring slavery that gave way to Jim
Crow laws, which turned into law and order.

The difference now is that law and
order were able to fool even the African
Americans; they welcomed it. They were
asking for more law enforcement to rid their
community of crimes. I would say, like the
Supreme Court ruling in 1968, "It reflects
custom and tradition, preserve public peace

and good order." That is what legal positivism does: takes something immoral and makes it acceptable because it is the law, when, in fact, law and morality are not two separate entities. Morality is the fundament of the law. When a law is passed to hurt a group of people, what happened to the morality of those enacting the law? At some point, they will become immoral.

The criminalization of drug usage during the crack pandemic promoted the over-policing of the Black neighborhood, which resulted in mass incarceration for profit. The economic factors behind mass incarceration in America made it clear why this wrong happens to African Americans. If we were to compare the crack pandemic to the opioid epidemic, the difference is clear. It has not been criminalized because of the demographic of the addicted that are mostly white, and it is treated as a health issue as it should. There is an increase in rehabilitation facilities to help those that have fallen victim to these substances.

Those men and women have a chance of beating this affliction and re-entering society as mother, father, college students, and workers, and have a second chance at life. That is the social privilege and distinction between White and Black in America. If only the African American were treated that way in the 80s, it would have been the perfect example of race equality when plagued with a drug pandemic. But instead, they were sent to jail and served longer sentences for minor violations without addressing the addiction. It would have been a moral duty to care for the community instead of treating them as criminals that needed to be arrested and imprisoned with a mandatory minimum sentence.

During the Obama administration, one of the changes made was to reduce sentences for nonviolent offenses. On May 10, 2017, Jeff Sessions, the US Attorney General at that time, in a memo to Federal prosecutors, changed the policy back to the mandatory minimum sentences, which usually resulted in the over-incarceration of minorities for minor, nonviolent crimes for an extended time. According to College Data, the average cost for college in 2019 is $26,590 for public and $53,980 for private for an academic year. Whereas in 2017, the Vera Institute of Justice released the average incarceration cost per inmate per year is about $31,000 nationwide, but in some states, it is about $60,000. Since taxpayers pay for the inmates, the money could have been put to better use.

According to *the New York Daily* news report, on January 17th, 2016, a 15-year-old honor roll student with no prior convictions in Georgia stole a pair of Nike sneakers worth about $100. The teen saw the shoes for sale on Facebook and contacted the seller. They met at the park. At the scene of the exchange, another man accompanied the teen and had a gun. When the man pulled the gun, they all fled. The teen said he did not know the person, and the seller could not identify the gunman. The teen stole the shoes. In May 2018, the teen was charged as an adult - five years in prison, and ten years of probation. The prosecutor called it a "break" for the teen because it was a lesser sentence from the ten years of prison time for armed robbery.

After serving five years in prison, even if the young man lives a pristine life, the likelihood of him not violating the ten-year probation that will send him back to jail is nearly impossible. Probation has so many rules. A walk in his neighborhood or a traffic stop, even a ride in a friend's car can send him back to jail for violating his probation. That is how you establish social control of a group to keep them locked up without a chance to re-enter society and be better citizens. Yes, a crime was committed, but did the punishment fit the crime? Slavery was immoral; Jim Crow laws were immoral; mandatory minimum sentences, law and order fueled by draconian and abusive laws that benefit political and financial gain; and promoted divisions are immoral as well.

If you think history does not repeat itself, think again. In 1933 when Hitler came to power, due to positive legalism in Germany, he was able to extend laws that prevented Jewish kids from going to school. In 1935, he went on to strip Jewish people that were born in Germany from their citizenship. He led a national boycott of Jewish businesses. He also requested that all Jewish people have a big J on their passport to identify them. Jewish citizens were harassed and subjected to violent attacks; stripped of their civil rights, they were no longer able to work government and professional jobs. They had to take menial jobs just to survive. They were arrested and put into camps. If they tried to leave the country, they had to remit 90% of their wealth as taxes, making them poor immigrants, and no country wanted to take them.

When mass deportation failed, in mid-1941, Hitler resorted to mass extermination. No one saw anything wrong with what he was doing from the start because it was the law. The Nazi Party advocated the concept of a Volksgemeinschaft (people community), which called all Germans to unity as national comrades, at the same time aiming to exclude people of another race that were a threat and could take over the county. The effect of his misguided unity is that 6 million people died, and no one said anything; because morality and the law were separated. Unjust laws are a distortion of the law and justice. As St. Thomas Aquinas put it: [7]"Positive law has as its purpose the common good of the community. Any positive law which conflicts/ is inconsistent with either natural law or divine law is not really law at all. Hence, not only is there no moral obligation to obey it, but there is no legal obligation to obey it, either."

America needs to wake up. We have African Americans being mass-incarcerated

---

[7] *Thomas Aquinas's Summa theologiae: A biography. Princeton University Press. McGinn, B. (2019).*

and dying at an alarming rate through gun violence. The police officers who took an oath to protect and serve are not all on board with keeping this oath; some of them are not even bothered to arrest Black people anymore. For example, in the George Floyd case, how do you put your knee on someone's neck for 8 minutes and 46 seconds, and not feel and hear life is leaving Mr. Floyd's body? We are only aware of the ones that make the news or social media.

The reality is Black lives are being destroyed and they are killed through gun violence, whether it is at the hand of the police or through their neighborhood. The neighborhoods can be safe; it has been proven through gentrification. That is another economic factor we will not talk about for now.

pg. 49 Guerdie Chery-Mesilas

PART III

INVISIBLE BIAS

"Love your neighbor as yourself."

[8](Mar 12:31 NIV)

---

[8] *Holy Bible, New International Version. Biblical Inc. Publishing House, 2011.*

The qualifications to be a racist are very simple and are outside of race and ethnicity. If you were born in America or live in America, go to school, and watched TV, two of the four things mentioned will qualify you to form opinions and stereotypes of any race or ethnic group without real facts. Therefore, that qualifies you to be a racist. That is why it is not OK to say you are not racist. You have to be anti-racism. Being anti-racism means there is an education process that must take place about any group before forming an opinion to dispel the stereotypes and address all the invisible biases engraved in our minds.

When looking at old footage of the civil rights movement, I often noticed children were part of the march, and children were part of the white people that were upset about the changes to their way of life. Have you ever wondered what happened to those children? The children on both sides become law-makers, government workers, doctors, lawyers, and other professions. One can only hope the Black children grew up to stay true to the cause of civil rights for all, and the White children rejected their parent's racist views. Unfortunately, some people have been breastfed the milk of racism when they cannot act on it; they applied invisible biases. It comes into play in the form of policy making, rules, and one-sided regulations, less opportunity, less service, lack of information.

In the workplace, they cannot overtly practice racism. Still, the invisible biases against Black people are there, meticulously put in place, in the form of rules and regulations that are one-sided and sometimes go unnoticed. Being black and a woman in the workplace is a second reason for discrimination. In 1962, Malcolm x stated, [9]"The most disrespected person in America is a black woman. The most unprotected person in America is the black woman. The most neglected person in American is the black woman." Black

---

[9] *Malcolm X's speech in Los Angeles, amara.org, 1962.*

women seemed to be an easy target with no recourse. All the negative attention of racism will be shifted to the Black woman before any other group.

At some point or another, African Americans experienced racism and were subjected to discriminatory practices that no one will ever believe happened, and they are unable to prove it. For instance, when a Black person walked into a store, suddenly, everyone seemed to be paying attention to only that person. It would not be wrong if it were to provide customer service, except it was not. They followed you on every aisle, asking the same questions. The same person is passing you every 30 seconds, asking, "Can I help you find anything" when they can see you are looking at that one item already in your hand. In other instances, when you go to some big chain stores with certain products under lock, you have to wait longer than most to get products that are used by Black women. When you go to a company, banks, or government offices, you are more likely to receive less information.

If you do not know what to ask, you are left uninformed. If you do ask, you still receive limited information. One example is that white teachers who already have the bias that Black students are less capable will not waste their time recommending them for gifted classes even if they are smart. The counselor will not provide all the information about how to get scholarships. The cycle goes on and on.

If you live in America, despite your best effort and intention, you could be seen as racist; that is why it is crucial to make it a personal effort to be anti-racist. We have been conditioned by propaganda to believe specific crimes and behaviors are associated with a group of people. That is why a White person will cling to her purse or cross the street to walk on the other side of the road when they see a Black person coming towards them. A White person will call the police because they see a Black person doing everyday tasks. They feel the need to call the police and report because, in the back of their mind, it is not normal, they might be here to commit a crime.

A story was brought to my attention about three young people. The year is 2020; the three kids grew up together, two young ladies about 17 years old and a young Black man 19 years old. I will identify them as Girl A White, Girl B White, and Boy C Black. The teens grew up together and attended the same school. Boy C is an athlete who graduated high school the year before and is now attending college. He started dating Girl A in high school; their parents are aware of the relationship and OK with it. The teens are friends and hang out together at times.

Girl B decided she wants to experiment with drugs or started to use drugs. One day, she decided to ask Boy C to buy it. He declined her request because he did not do drugs and did not want to buy drugs. She was upset and told him that if he did not do it, she would call the cops on him, and tell them he was a drug dealer and a rapist because her friend Girl A was 17 and he was 19. Upon hearing the comment, Girl A was horrified and reported the incident to her parents and decided to stop being friends with Girl B. She was not aware her friend was a drug user and was bent on getting her boyfriend in trouble.

Their parents are not racist; they are regular everyday people that faced the same challenges that we all experience and are trying to do the right thing. The question is what makes a 17-year-old white girl think she can threaten a 19-year-old Black man of being a rapist and a drug dealer if he does not do her bidding?

The reality is she knew the current climate, and most likely, the young Black man would get arrested and questioned even if a lie was being told. She knew she had the power to do so and would be believed. Was she racist? After all, they were friends. Was she just a drug addict ready to do anything to get her next fix? They are no longer friends, and that is a relief for all the parents involved; whichever way you look at this situation, it is not suitable for either one of them. I hope the young lady gets the help she needs before it is too late. I am also glad the young Black man involved did not have to experience the effect of her lies because his girlfriend did not take the threat too lightly and informed her parents, who advised the other parents of the situation.

I recall my brother was about 15 years old. He started wearing baggy clothes and braided his hair. My mother was furious because he went for that style. She told him about all the things she had seen on TV about young Black men and how they were treated based on their looks. She told him he should not dress a certain way because appearances do matter. Like a teenager in his infinite wisdom, he did not listen to her and kept his hairstyle and baggy clothes. Our neighborhood was pretty safe and low-key.

One day as he was coming from school, He approached an older lady that lived in the same apartment complex for years and used to babysit him as a child and my brother sometimes walked her dog. She was a lovely old lady. On that day, she came out to walk her dog. She saw this young Black man coming toward her; she started running and calling for help. My teenage brother and his protective instinct, without thinking or looking back to see what was behind him, quickly grabbed her arm and scooped the little dog off the floor to get them through the gate and closed it as fast as he could. While he was doing that, he called out her name, and she recognized his voice, and she said my brother's name and asked if that was him. My brother looked around and noticed there was no one else behind him. My brother called her by her name again and asked what was wrong, who was coming to attack them. She said to him she did not recognize him coming towards her. She apologized to him and said she noticed it was him when he said her name, so she stopped screaming. She looked at him and rubbed his head and said, "You almost gave me a heart attack. Why did you change your hair, and why are you dressed in those big clothes? I thought you were coming to rob me." My 15-year-old brother exclaimed, "I thought you saw someone behind me with a gun or something. You scared me too."

My brother then questioned why his looks alone from afar gave someone that knew him the impression he was a robber without saying or committing any action that would indicate robbery. He went to the barbershop the next day, cut his hair, and slowly changed his style in clothing. My mother saw the changes. At first, she thought her words got through to him until he told her what had happened. He was so ashamed of it; he waited a few days to say it to us. Upon hearing the news, my mother was more concerned about the old lady's eyesight than of racism because she had known her for a long time.

Was the old white lady racist? She has been conditioned to believe a look is associated with certain behaviors, and she fell for it. I realized that day that she took my brother's creativity, his sense to experiment with style to know how he wanted to dress, and what he wanted to do with his hair. His innocence about style was taken away that day. But other young Black men were not so lucky. Some experienced police harassment, brutality, arrests, imprisonment, and even died because of this misconception.

I recall when my son was in elementary school, we were doing his homework, but we usually stop and glance at the 6:00 p.m. news mostly to see how the weather was going to be the next day. There was a news flash about an arrest, showing mug shots after mug shots of young Black men that were arrested that day. My son asked why were only Black men on the news for doing bad things? I realized I made a mistake. Why did I let him see that news? Then I also realized this was a teachable moment. I explained to him there are other people committing crimes as well. The Black men were paraded on the news because the media wants us to think and believe they were the only ones committing crimes.

I went on the police website to show him the arrests in our county for the day and a week. We watched the 6:00 p.m. news for a week, and I let him ask questions. Every evening, a couple of young Black men were on the news for some type of crime. Sometimes minor and sometimes significant, but it looked as if the daily goal was to present that image every day. At the same time, I would go on the police website that showed the number of arrests for the day, and we looked through them. There were some other crimes, and they were not all committed by Black men. We would find some that we thought should have been on the news for public awareness; however, the other criminals did not make the news because they did not fit the profile of what we were supposed to see and understand.

Just like dishonest scholarship was a tool used to validate slavery on the concept that Black people were somewhat mentally deficient and more related to monkeys than to humans, it was the propaganda of the time. The same thing happens to the media propaganda of young Black men being violent. They have been paraded every day in the news for committing crimes. If you control the story and the narrative of what you want people to think is a problem, you will succeed at creating biases against that particular group of people, and it transcends race, gender, and ethnicity. Everyone, even members of the same group of people, will start thinking these people are a problem, and the collective that is not the problem should find a solution. There is a system that sells racism, and it is counting on the miseducation of everyone for it to work. In reality, we are all victims of the same system in one way or another.

Once at work, a very misinformed co-worker decided to comment about Haiti's political instability because they were on the news trying to remove a freely elected president. We were all watching the same news; however, the question was directed at me specifically. Why are the Haitians so uncivilized that they are unable to self-govern? I was asked the question because I was Haitian. I wanted to point out how offensive and disrespectful the question was, but I knew better than going that route. Instead, I smiled and replied, "When you make an effort to know about Haitian history, you will earn the right to ask about why they are uncivilized and unable to self-govern."

The fact is the tumultuous situation is deeply rooted in the history of the nation, and what was happening was the direct result of being the first free democratic Black nation that wanted to self-govern. A system was designed around Haiti that reduced its people into poverty, uneducated people that are unable to unite and self-govern.

Suppose you are reading this book and ask how so. Please allow me to explain. I was born and raised in Haiti and was taught Haitian history as a child and throughout my young adult life. Africa, which is where our ancestors came from, was not the main subject of our studies. I had to memorize the Haitian history book for years; I remembered it briefly talked about the Natives that occupied the land and the arrival of the Europeans that resulted in the Africans being brought to the island to replace the natives that died of harsh labor and diseases. African history for me started with the transatlantic ships that transported the slaves. I do not recall Africa being mentioned as a continent with various independent countries or tribes with different cultures and clear social distinctions. Those depictions were not there; we had no idea what was going on in Africa at that time, why other Africans sold their African brothers for bottles, hats, and spoons. No information on the tribes that resisted and fought the slave runners. A nation with no roots to go back to and mistrusted each other. There is a Haitian saying that goes "depi nan ginen neg trahi neg," meaning "Blacks betraying Blacks started in the Guinea." Throughout the nation's history, the mistrust is present. It is only through personal growth that I learned more about the continent of Africa prior to slavery, which I encourage everyone to do. Also read books like: *"Stolen legacy,"* *"Ethiopia and the Origin of Civilization"*.

The Haitian revolution is the most misrepresented historical account in the history of revolutions. So much so, after the earthquake in 2010 that devasted the country and killed so many of its people, one evangelical pastor got on the news and said the Haitians made a pact with the devil; that is why Haiti has been the way it is, and that is why the earthquake happened and killed so many of them. I was furious that a man of God would make these comments during a tragedy when people will look to the body of Christ for consolation. He has a right to his opinion, but when you are in a position of leadership, your opinion can be detrimental. It would have been useful to know what he was trying to accomplish with the comment he made. I was sure it was not to bring people closer to Christ.

On January 14th, 2010, I decided to send the beloved pastor a quick email. It came from the pain I was experiencing, because I was going out of my mind if I did not put it in writing. Below is what I wrote to him.

Dear Pastor

Many Haitians are Christians and praying to Jehovah God. As a man of God, your knowledge about curses and blessing seems to be limited, you should have known that Jesus died on the cross two thousand years ago and shed his blood for all nations. "For God so loved the world, that he gave his only begotten Son, that whosoever believeth in him should not perish, but have everlasting life." John 3:16 King James Bible. Whatever pact you think the Haitians made with the devil two hundred years ago, once they have come to know the Lord Jesus, that curse has been lifted, and they are free. God was on his throne the day of the deluge, and he is still on his throne now. Certain things are not for us to understand why; God is almighty, all-knowing. Your comment is offensive because, in a way, it justified slavery as a God-given right just as they believed it back then. Maybe you should read more about what these people were subjected to during the time of slavery that united them in their broken dialect to revolt the way they did. They needed something to believe in, and the god your ancestors were offering them was the same one that wanted to keep them as slaves. Dear Pastor, I am now offering you to take the Lord Jesus as your savior; please make peace with him. Because whenever you make an offensive comment that hurts other human beings, you do it to Jesus. You are not a good witness to his loving teaching. You have worked too hard for God; please do take these comments to heart before making them not for another person or me but for Jesus. My dad and two brothers are missing. I always watch your show for inspiration and comfort, but on that day, I felt devastated more by your comment than the fact that I was still unable to contact them.

I am pretty sure I was not the only person that wrote him and was furious at his comment. A few days later, his ministry issued an apology on the news.

I am not romanticizing Haitian history: just like every nation it has the good, bad, and ugly—the greedy, corrupt, patriotic, and civil rights seekers. Haiti is the first country in the Americas to abolish slavery, and became the first Black nation. After the brutal war concluded, they proceeded to murder all of the French residents of all ages. The exception was the Polish soldiers who defected, German colonists, medical doctors, and professionals whose skills they needed to rebuild the country. Revolution and war are messy. The genocide of the French residents was the reaction of centuries of brutalities against slaves, and they learned it from the French Revolution.

A white nation fights for their independence; it is a beautiful thing to be celebrated. The American Revolution, which followed and inspired the French Revolution, were both fought against oppression and injustice, and they were violent. The Haitian Revolution was not different, except it was a Black nation. After they gained their independence, they went around helping other countries fight for their freedom. The Haitian revolt facilitated the

Louisiana purchase. The question again was, why are they unable to self-govern?

In the 1700s, Haiti had over 450 thousand slaves. The island was one of the wealthiest countries in the world, supporting France's economy. The slaves of Haiti revolted and fought against the Napoleon troops, one of the most powerful armies in the world. On January 1st, 1804, they proclaimed their independence after a 13-year long revolt. Due to the French menace of re-invasion, Haiti agreed to pay reparations for lost property to the slave owners. That property was the slaves.

In addition to a 21-billion-dollar independence debt, Haiti was also forced to sell their product at 50% off to France, which was the only country willing to buy from them. There was an international boycott on commerce with Haiti. The Haitian government took loans with interest from banks to pay the debt. It was paid off in 1947. It was at the expense of education, health care, and infrastructures for the new nation. The Haitians were free but enslaved by debt. Meanwhile, France abolished slavery in 1848. But the banks still wanted their money. Haiti was the first and only nation forced to pay an indemnity to the people who enslaved them. In 2004, the Haitian government asked for the repayment of that money. In 2015, the French president said the only thing they owed Haiti was a moral debt, and refused to repay the money.

Haiti's struggle with development and a stable government is due to foreign power intervention, ignorance, and poverty. The majority of the nation is illiterate, crippled by poverty, and ruined by corruption. Due to regional and commercial interests, in 1915, the United States invaded Haiti. The small island was caught between Germany and the United States, who integrated and destabilized its political and financial course. Both countries understood the strategic importance of the island in workforce, materials, wealth, and port facilities in the lead up to World War I.

Haiti had a period of political instability between 1911 and 1915; seven presidents were assassinated or overthrown. The German citizens integrated by inter-marrying and having children to get around the laws of the land. They financed many of the political unrest by giving loans at high interest to opposing parties. The United States integrated by controlling the economy, and the government by putting poppet presidents. The United States was displeased with the Germans; they were being hostile and threatened their interests in Haiti.

On January 27th, 1914, the USS *Montana* disembarked in Port au Prince; that was the first part of the invasion. The only commercial bank in the country was The Bank National of Haiti, which served as the Haitian government's treasury, was acquired by the United States through Citibank, and in December 1914, Haiti's gold reserve was transferred to the National Citibank in New York for safe-keeping.

On July 28th, 1915, following the murder of the Haitian President Vilbrun Guillaume, the United States President

Woodrow Wilson ordered the invasion to protect American and foreign interest. The mission was to establish peace; it ended on August 1st, 1934. It took nineteen years to establish peace. The United States forgot that the French colony help finance its revolution. The Haitians helped the United States with their independence in 1779, when, at the battle of Savannah, "Chasseurs Volontaires," Infantry Volunteers, a group of Haitians, volunteered to fight to help the cause of freedom.

The occupation changed the education system from the liberal arts inherited from the French to vocational training similar to the United States for minorities and immigrants. The occupation had some positive effects, like stabilizing the Haitian currency, improving the infrastructure, and hospitals construction. However, there were also some negative effects of the occupation. The infrastructures and hospitals were improved through forced labor known as civil conscription, which led to the mass murder of innocent civilians. It also brought racism and turned the Black nation into a second-class global citizen.

Some Haitians resisted the invasion. They were called the Cacos. By 1920, they were gone because they lost their so-called allied Germany after the 1st world war ended. There were a series of puppet governments put in place by the United States. It also gave rise to thousands of Haitians migrating to the Dominican Republic and Cuba. In 1918, the Haitian constitution was rewritten, allowing foreigners to purchase land, which was forbidden by the founding fathers after gaining their independence in 1804.

During the occupation, 40% of Haiti's national income was designated to repay debts to American and French banks; this froze Haiti's economic development. Haiti's economy was still controlled by the United States 10 years after the occupation. Instead of peace, the occupation left a blueprint for more oppressors and totalitarian regimes to this day. They learned how to dominate by using intimidation, repression, corruption, bribery, extortion, and stolen government funds. Haiti is still in poverty; this is the highest form of slavery.

Haiti has been and remained strategically important. It has been used as a counterbalance against communist Cuba and is located in the middle of the war on drugs. Haiti's geographical position has not changed; it is still part of the Windward Passage (Canal du Vent), which is a strait that connects the Caribbean Sea to the Atlantic Ocean. A stable government would be in the nation's best interest; the massive deforestation that caused more natural disasters to occur could have been prevented. Stable government would establish control and regulation of natural resources that are exploited out of Haiti and regulations of maritime and airspace. Haiti faces the challenging issues of human trafficking, mostly children and human organs and child prostitution. Why would a nation not want peace and control of its border?

Haiti has not been able to self-govern because it is the first free Black republic; the many vested interests along with corrupt leaders will not let it happen. To put Haiti's political instability in perspective for a better understanding of its current social and economic problems: from 1804 to 2020, Haiti had 42 head of state or presidents. Of the 42 head of state, the current president included, 9 presidents finished their term, and 32 did not complete their term. Those that did not complete their term, some died while in power, were assassinated, or overthrown. Religion has not been much help either. Some people have been taught by others who chose to misrepresent God's word that their homes are in heaven; they did not need to be part of the earthly government, so most of the time they do not vote. Corrupt and incompetent leaders grab power and do what they do best.

The story of Haiti should be a familiar one to people of African descent. It is prevalent for them to experience the following: a people held hostage and kidnapped, to have countries' economies built on their backs and the back of their descendants while still not being part of the very society they helped to build. In terms of wealth, education, and social status, they are always at the bottom and living in poverty. In the word of Edward E. Baptist, [10]"The commodification and suffering and forced labor of the African Americans are what made the United States powerful and rich."

---

[10] *Baptist, E. E. (2016) The Half has never been told: Slavery and the making of American capitalism. (Basic Books)*

pg. 78 Guerdie Chery-Mesilas

PART IV

CASUAL

RACISM

"Whoever sows injustice reaps calamity, and the rod they wield in fury will be broken."

[11](Proverbs 22:8 NIV)

---

[11] *Holy Bible, New International Version. Biblical Inc. Publishing House, 2011.*

There are two sides to casual racism; people sometimes do it unknowingly and other times with malice. It can be challenging to differentiate the two, especially if the outcome is the same. People experience it differently on different levels. Avoidance is not the answer because it is nearly impossible to see it coming.

Casual racism is often done in a way that the person doing it may know what they are doing and can be explicit, but do not want to be seen as racist. For instance, in the workplace, there are rules against racist behavior and action, but racism casually done can go undetected and blame the victim of being too sensitive or angry. One of the reasons is preconceiving notions about this particular group and stereotypes deeply rooted in the culture. Another reason is just a lack of respect for the person; therefore, the racists will do whatever it takes to make the person feel unwelcome and like they do not belong. The racists do not care how it will affect the person. They cannot be bothered with such a person's feelings, needs, and future. Since racism is not tolerated, they will find ways to manipulate situations or events to make sure their story is the one that is believed after they hurt the person.

They also know they will have the backing of whomever the issue is reported to because, after all, everyone can identify with someone who says or uses specific keywords: I was afraid, I fear for my safety. They believe they have moral superiority, and they are doing a service to get rid of the issue or the person. They use that knowledge to manipulate situations and instill fear. There is no cure for this type of racists. You have a person who knowingly discriminates against others and gets away with it. If you happened to be their victim, the only thing that can help is when you have proof of their action. For instance, the constant calling of 911 on Black people; to report what they are doing, which is usually normal activities. It is merely due to the fact a Black person is doing it. In the racist mind, a Black person has to be up to no good.

Due to technological advancement, we are now seeing racists on social media. More and more people are recording and posting their interactions with racists, but these things are not new; they have been happening for years. A walk or run around your neighborhood, in the park, swimming in a pool, and other normal activities warrant a phone call to the police to check this Black person. Remind them of their place, or embarrass them when they know the situation can escalate into something else. The goal is to see Black people under the full force of the law to maintain good order, sometimes with no due diligence to see if they have the right person before applying the full force of the law.

One of my sisters, her husband, and my younger brother, who reside in Boston, traveled to Florida for a weekend to visit Universal Studios. They arrived at the FLL airport, picked up their rental car, and were on their way to Orlando. They got on the highway I95 going north; they were listening to music, not paying much attention around them. They passed West Palm Beach, and as soon as they entered Jupiter, FL, her husband, who was the driver, noticed a police car behind them. He changed lane, giving way to the emergency vehicle, thinking the police car might want to go faster. The police car merged to the lane as well and remained behind him.

He told his wife and his brother-in-law, "I think we are going to be pulled over, because there is a police vehicle tailing me, so stay calm." My sister, who was in the front passenger seat, replied, "Make sure you do the speed limit, so we do not get a ticket." At the same time, my younger brother, who was in the back seat, noticed a helicopter above the highway. He jokingly said, "This helicopter has been hovering above us for a while. What if this helicopter was here for us?" My sister and her husband laughed.

My brother-in-law noticed two more police vehicles, one to his left and one to his right. He told my brother there was probably an accident ahead and the police was responding to it, because he could see a lot of lights ahead. A few seconds later, all the police vehicles turned on their lights and sirens. My brother-in-law put on his signal to merge to the right lane so he could pull over. The police vehicle would not let that happen, so my sister told him to slow way down until he could stop. That is when he noticed the highway was empty. It was just their car and the police vehicles that accompanied them, and up ahead, there was a barricade cutting off the highway, full of police cars and special unit trucks.

He immediately stopped the car a few feet short of the barricades. Suddenly, at least a dozen police officers moved towards the car with guns drawn. The police officers outside of the car were screaming obscenities to get them to open the car doors, lower the windows, and put their hands up. My family members did not know which command to obey, so they all put their hands up. My sister began to scream hysterically. My brother later told me the police officers all looked nervous, especially a young-looking red-headed officer whose hand was shaking as he pointed the gun at my brother. At this point, my family members all feared getting shot. The police were hitting the car windows with their guns. My brother-in-law, while screaming, "I am unlocking the door," closed his fist, keeping one finger up, and slowly moved it toward the car door to unlock it. As soon as the door clicked, he was pulled out of the vehicle to the ground. My sister was still screaming and unresponsive to the commands of the police likely in shock. From the back seat, my brother noticed his sister was not complying and seemed to be in shock, so he started saying very loudly and slowly, "I'm going to unbuckle her seatbelt, I'm going to unbuckle her seatbelt." My brother very slowly, as he was repeating himself very loudly, began reaching with one finger, first up in the air, then in a downward motion to the seat belt lock. He unbuckled his sister's seatbelt, then unbuckled his own.

My sister told me she does not
remember much of how she got out of the
car, except that she heard the click
unlocking the car doors and felt herself
being pulled out of the car with a lot of force
and slammed to the ground. I was on my
belly with four officers kneeling on me. As I
moved my head, I saw my husband and
brother pinned to the ground, and police
officers were on top of them." She said her
husband, later on, reported that as soon as he
was slammed to the ground, he quickly put
his hands behind his back, and one officer
said to him, "I see you've done this before;
you know exactly which position to take." I
should also mention that at the time of this
event, my sister was six months pregnant
with her first child. My brother and brother-
in-law kept asking the police officers to
handcuff my sister with her hands in front of
her and not behind her back because she was
pregnant but were ignored.

They were questioned with guns
pointing at them after they were handcuffed
and moved to the side of the highway.

"Where are you coming from? Where are you going? What is in the car?" All their answers were the same. "We flew in this morning from Boston to Fort Lauderdale, picked up a rental car, and we are driving to Orlando to go to Universal Studios."

"What is in the car?"

"Our bags are in the car."

"What is in the bags?"

"Our clothes for the weekend."

The vehicle was searched, and their bags too. They were all placed in the backseat of one police car with the windows rolled up in the summer heat of Florida. The space was so tight in the backseat, their knees were hunched up close to their chest and touched the barrier between the front and back seats.

The only thing they heard coming from the officers' mouth was that "we got them," but still no explanation about why they were violently arrested. My youngest brother explained to one of the officers who came to his car to retrieve something that my sister was six months pregnant; if they kept her in that hot car, she would throw up. Then the officer went over and cracked one of the windows. About 30 minutes later, they brought in an older white man and kept him at a distance. They pulled my brother-in-law out of the car and lined him up on the side of the highway with officers surrounding him. The older white man shook his head as a sign for no.

Another 30 minutes went by before a white man wearing a suit came and instructed the officers to release them. After they removed the handcuffs, my sister asked why were they violently handcuffed and detained? The man glanced back at them and said they had a home invasion with an armed robbery committed by two Black men that got away in a white vehicle traveling southbound. Recall that my family members were traveling northbound, the opposite direction. My sister replied to the police officer that this car had three people, two Black men and one Black woman. The police officer did not answer. She asked what type of white car because this car was a rental. He told her, "we know," and walked away. No apology, no explanation.

They were numb and stood on the side of the highway with the bags that were in the car now on the ground with all their belongings scattered. The police officers left the scene so fast, my sister did not even have time to request their names and badge numbers. They continued to drive to Orlando; not a word was exchanged among them until they made it to the park. They asked each other what in the world just happened to us. All the praying mothers and grandmothers in the family knew it was only by divine intervention that they were not assassinated on the highway. My sister did not visit Florida again for a long time, and when she mustered the courage to visit, she would not drive or rent a car.

The other side of casual racism is when it is done by people who may not even be aware that they are racist. They did not intend to; it is because no thought was put into the action or words being said. They jokingly say something they had no idea you should not say to a particular individual and do not understand why it is offensive. Someone can tell a racially charged joke, but you, who identifies with the group or know people from this particular group, did not find it funny, and no one seems to understand why it was not funny. For instance, saying Happy Columbus Day to a Native American or African American may not be the best thing to say to them because we are looking at the history behind the holiday celebration from different perspectives.

The white perspective is America's discovery; it is a great day that opened the door to a new world and wealth. The Native American perspective is that it is a horrible day that reminds them of how a nation was deceived, pillaged, and resulted in the genocide of Native Americans. The African American perspective is that it represents over 300 years of brutal slavery, continuous oppression, and the fight for civil rights.

There is hope for this particular type of casual racism, and it is fixable. This person may be culturally illiterate, and that is why they say certain things. The person can get educated on races, traditions, and customs of other people. They are usually open to know why it was offensive, especially if they did not mean to offend others.

pg. 93 Guerdie Chery-Mesilas

PART V

POVERTY

BY

DESIGN

"Whoever oppresses the poor shows contempt for their maker, but whoever is kind to the needy honors God."

[12](Proverbs 14:31 NIV)

---

[12] *Holy Bible, New International Version. Biblical Inc. Publishing House, 2011.*

There are several extraordinary men and women, both Black and White, who understood the issues faced by Black people both then and now. They have devoted their lives and lost their lives for the cause. There is one challenge that has always been at the center of it all, and it is poverty. When it strikes the Black community, it tends to stay for generation after generation because of systemic rules put in place to keep them in poverty. Poverty does not discriminate; it affects all races and comes to kill, steal, and destroy.

Poverty is intertwined with crime. Poor neighborhoods are usually plagued with drugs and crime. You do not need to be a genius to understand that poverty promotes crime. The fact is if someone is not a psychopath who has an urge to commit crimes, the other explanation is as simple as there is a need that was not met, which creates the perfect setting for criminal activities. Young people, because of a lack of reason, lack of basic necessities, and bad influences, fall prey and are pushed to commit crimes. Older people commit crimes for the same reasons, or they have bad habits or are stuck in a system with no way out. If you are in a position of power and can make a difference, you simply need a good heart to do so.

Poverty affects people in ways that are unimaginable and changes their perspective on life. A single mom that makes minimum wage is a poor person. She will have to choose between feeding her children or paying rent. Buying clothes and the latest gear is a luxury she cannot afford. If she has to work two jobs to make ends meet, the children she cares about are being raised by the TV or the neighborhood full of people that are one way or another victim of the same cycle of poverty. The perception that there is no other way to get what you want, especially if you are unemployable, is to commit crimes, is prevalent. Men were not supposed to be out of work. Nothing good comes from boredom. There is an old saying, "Idle hands are the devil's workshop."

African Americans were never intended to be part of the American Society. So much so that immigrants from European countries came in and were welcomed. Even if the first generation had a hard time, by the second generation, they were fully integrated and were now the ones discriminating against the Blacks because that was the norm. When hand outs are given to white people, it is a subsidy or bail out. But to Black people, it is welfare. Systemic racism in government creates a different world for African Americans, and it functions differently for them on how they can acquire government assistance for basic necessities.

A society is a group of people that agree to do things and abide by certain rules for mutual benefits, like safety, security, and prosperity. That has not been the case for African Americans. There is no safety, security, and prosperity in the rules for the Black people. The very rules encourage crimes, and crime in America is a business.

If crimes cease in America, there are a few industries that will cease to exist.

The cost of living has increased so many times, yet the minimum wage has not improved much. It is a fight to change that because it will affect the bottom line of big corporations. The poverty that pushes someone to commit crimes and become a felon does not disappear after they served the sentence. When they get out of prison, the situation that put them there is waiting for them. It gets more complicated because most companies do not hire felons, and they are not eligible for government assistance like food stamps and housing. Those are basic necessities, so what is that person to do other than commit more crimes that put them in the same mass incarceration for profit. You have fathers meeting their sons in jail, sometimes two to three generations of men and women stuck in the same cycle of crime and poverty in and out jail.

African Americans, after 300 years of slavery and 60-plus years of oppression, were never integrated into the system to be

part of the society they helped to build. If
they were, the rules would have been
different. A group of people that were not
educated on how to function and were
treated like cattle or property needed to be
educated, prepared on how to function, and
become productive members of that society.
Instead, they were always seen as a means
of exploitation or something to get rid of if it
cannot be exploited. Their children are not
seen as kids but little criminals that need to
be tamed and contained. When mass
incarceration failed, mass murder is the
option, which is what is happening with all
the shootings. A minor traffic violation, a
run in your neighborhood, a trip to the
corner store, all can become a deadly
encounter.

Every race has criminals, and people
commit crimes where they live. If you
commit a crime, you should go to jail, and
the punishment should fit the crime. But as a
society, we should not have a system that is
not even trying to keep the honest man

honest. The disproportionate arrest and killing of African Americans is wrong.

The lesson is simple: if it is unjust, not right, not fair, do something about it. Whether it is happening to you or others, fight it as if your very survival depends on it, because it might just be true for the affected party.

pg. 102 Guerdie Chery-Mesilas

PART VI

THE

GUIDE

"Above all else, guard your heart, for everything you do flows from it." [13](Proverbs 4:23 NIV)

---

[13] *Holy Bible, New International Version. Biblical Inc. Publishing House, 2011.*

Due to a lifetime of advertising campaigns and upside-down propaganda that dictate that based on what certain people look like, they must be associated with crimes, the idea has been seared in our minds. We cannot help but to be suspicious or make comments or act a certain way that will offend others. Below is a list of things that might be useful. They can be used not to assume the worst of each other, because most Black people are not criminals and do not want to be bothered.

- When you see a Black person with a lot of cash: do not assume they are drug dealers. If you see a white person with a lot of cash, what is your first instinct? How much cash are we talking about that raised your suspicions?

- If you find yourself with an urge to do the right thing: look within and ask yourself if that right thing is not intentionally trying to hurt someone based on their looks.

- If you feel the need to call the police
  on someone: check to see if you need
  to mind your business. Is there a
  crime that needs to be reported?

- If you feel like Black people should
  not be where you are: since you are
  uncomfortable with their presence,
  just leave. Do not try to get them to
  leave or make them uncomfortable
  by questioning if they should be
  there. They paid just like you to be
  where they are.

- If you want drugs: do not ask the
  first Black person you see if they
  have drugs or sell drugs.

- If you feel the need to give a
  compliment to a Black person: let it
  come from the heart; make sure it is
  not racially charged.

- If a Black person walks into your store or business: do not change the price to overcharge them.

- If you do not know why certain black people act a certain way: do not ask a Black person to help you understand. We do not know either.

- If you went to the beach and have a suntan: do not tell a black person "I am almost as black as you."

- If you are having a bad day and go on a racist rampage: telling Black people you have Black friends, or your boyfriend/husband or girlfriend/wife or kids are black is not a license.

The normal routine and daily encounter of a Black person differs from the White person on so many levels. The assumption is that white is right, and if you are black, you must be up to no good; therefore, must be watched and questioned.

The daily hostility alone is enough to drive one to madness, and it is the very foundation for racism that promotes systemic violence against Black people.

The normalization of insanity and insane behavior is far too common for Black people. The African Americans were not involved so they can learn, and in turn, teach their children. The forefathers hypocritical stand failed to include the Black people. Thank God for this generation of men and women that get it and will change it.

pg. 109 Guerdie Chery-Mesilas

<u>**EPILOGUE**</u>

I wrote this book because of how my family members and I experienced casual racism and invisible biases. In some instances, it was deliberate with malicious intent, and in other cases, it was merely at the right place at the wrong time or pure bad luck. The fact remained the intent in almost every case was a lack of respect or regard for us as human beings, people with rights deserving better treatment.

The stories did not end badly, but the emotional scars are rooted so deeply that it shaped our opinions and views. The stories, as I have been told, ended on a positive note for us that is in comparison to the usual sad, heartbreaking news that we become accustomed to seeing on the news or social media.

Unfortunately, the current climate is a complicated situation that affects minorities all over the world, not just

America. I call it poverty and injustice by design. It helps control the minority groups within a population. Changes will occur, and they have to - that is the only way of moving forward. It will require an individual effort combined with systematic changes within the society.

It is really up to an individual to get educated about race, generational, and systematic disadvantages to a group and choose to do better. It is also an individual effort to find out how your group was unjustly, disadvantageously treated, and educate yourself on how you are going to rise above the challenges and raise your children to do better and be better.

As a collective, it is up to us to make changes to become conscientious about how we want our government to operate for us. After all, America is a democratic country, where people vote, and elect politicians to serve the people. People with a platform, whether it is politics, social media, music,

and movies, have a responsibility to become
more socially responsible in what they do
and promote. We have to do better in our
community and by our community.

Social responsibility goes a long
way, and should start at home with family
and friends. We have a responsibility to
raise our children to become decent people
with good manners and proper ethical
values. We do have Black and White
families doing just that. However, the most
prominent social changes need to happen
with the lawmakers that are writing and
enacting laws based on profit for
corporations instead of the common good of
the people. If social justice is not in place,
the disadvantaged group will always be
victimized.

Until each one of us realizes how we
benefitted and the part we played in the
system that caused the economic disparity
that promotes poverty and crime, which also
creates a vicious cycle for the minorities, no

changes can be accomplished. [14]"The needs
of a society determine its ethics." Maya
Angelou.

---

[14] *Angelou, Maya (2010). Know why the caged bird sings. Random House.*

pg. 114 Guerdie Chery-Mesilas

If you have ever been discriminated against or experience casual racism and would like to share your story, please email me.
casualracisminamerica@gmail.com

[15]"My story was not meant for me alone. My story was given to me to help others." Dru Nicolas Vernet

After reading this book, if you realize you have discriminated against others and would like to share your story or need help to do better, please email me.
casualracisminamerica@gmail.com

---

[15] *Dru Nicolas Vernet (2020) - Truth and Triumph.*

pg. 116 Guerdie Chery-Mesilas

<u>**Works Cited**</u>

Processing anger: A conversation with Dr. Maya Angelou & Dave Chappelle. (2016, December 15). Medialectic. https://medialectic.wordpress.com/2016/12/15/processing-anger-a-conversation-with-dr-maya-angelou-dave-chappelle/

Angelou, M. (1970). I know why the caged bird sings. Random House.

How much does college cost? (n.d.). CollegeData. https://www.collegedata.com/en/pay-your-way/college-sticker-shock/how-much-does-college-cost/whats-the-price-tag-for-a-college-education/

European colonization of the Americas. (2002, May 19). Wikipedia, the free encyclopedia. Retrieved from https://en.wikipedia.org/wiki/European_colonization_of_the_Amer icas

Transatlantic slave trade | History & facts. (n.d.). Encyclopedia Britannica. https://www.britannica.com/topic/transatlantic-slave-trade

Atlantic slave trade. (2002, April 13). Wikipedia, the free encyclopedia. Retrieved from https://en.wikipedia.org/wiki/Atlantic_slave_trade

Baptist, E. E. (2016). The half has never been told: Slavery and the making of American capitalism. Basic Books.

The M.L. King speech. (n.d.). https://www.gphistorical.org/mlk/mlkspeech/

Slaves and the courts, 1740-1860. (n.d.). Library of Congress. https://www.loc.gov/teachers/classroommaterials/connections/slav es-court/file.html

United States occupation of Haiti En.wikipedia.org.
https://en.wikipedia.org/wiki/United_States_occupation_of_Haiti

Brown v. Board: When the Supreme Court ruled against segregation - National Constitution Center. (n.d.). National Constitution Center – constitutioncenter.org. https://constitutioncenter.org/blog/on-this-day-the-supreme-court-rules-against-segregation.

Capitalism. (2001, October 14). Wikipedia, the free encyclopedia. Retrieved from https://en.wikipedia.org/wiki/Capitalism

Richard Nixon. (n.d.). Encyclopedia Britannica. https://www.britannica.com/biography/Richard-Nixon

U.S. Senator Cory Booker of New Jersey. (2017, June 7). U.S. Senator Cory Booker of New Jersey. https://www.booker.senate.gov/news/press/booker-lee-durbin-paul-send-bipartisan-letter-questioning-new-charging-and-sentencing-policy-announced-by-ag-sessions

How much does it cost to send someone to prison? (2019, April 29). Marketplace. https://www.marketplace.org/2017/05/19/how-much-does-it-cost-send-someone-prison/

Schladebeck, J. (2018, June 2). Georgia teen with no record sentenced to five years in jail for stealing $100 sneakers. nydailynews.com. https://www.nydailynews.com/news/ny-news-teen-sentenced-five-years-stealing-sneakers-20180602-story.html

Adolf Hitler's rise to power. (2006, January 21). Wikipedia, the free encyclopedia. Retrieved from https://en.wikipedia.org/wiki/Adolf_Hitler%27s_rise_to_power.

McGinn, B. (2019). Thomas Aquinas's Summa theologiae: A biography. Princeton University Press.

pg. 119 Guerdie Chery-Mesilas

Guerdie Chery-Mesilas

I am a granddaughter, daughter, niece, cousin, sister, wife, mother, daughter-in-law, aunt, coworker, colleague, church member, Sunday school teacher. I am all these things to many people. What affects me affects them too. They turn around to put out the same energy to the rest of their world. The cycle goes on and on. We are connected, we are one, and we are the Church of Christ. Our job as the church is to speak the truth and bring hope.

I was born and raised in Haiti. I came to America when I was 21 years old. As an immigrant, I had to balance work and school and later family. I have a bachelor's degree in Hospitality Management and Travel and Tourism from Florida International University. I have a master's degree in Business Management from Fitchburg University. I love to read and enjoy long walks at the beach.

www.ingramcontent.com/pod-product-compliance
Lightning Source LLC
Chambersburg PA
CBHW031242250726
48655CB00005B/2053